Images From God

40 Devotions
to Encounter God's Heart

emmane

Dawn Hamsher

Dawn Hamsher

Cover Design - Marcy Rossi from FlyingPigFactory.com
Cover Artwork - Dawn Hamsher

Paperback ISBN: 978-1-959290-00-1
eBook ISBN: 978-1-959290-01-8

http://ekklesiaarising.co

Acknowledgments

I will give thanks to you, LORD, with all my heart…
Psalm 9:1 NIV

To God, above all, I thank You. There are no words that can adequately express the gratitude of my heart to You, my All-In-All. Thank You for being a God of relationship and for leading and guiding me on this (and every) journey!

These are the people who chase after Him…
Psalm 24:6 VOICE

To "My Girls" – Stephanie Gossert, Sandy James, and Trish Corbert, thank you for locking arms with me. Who else could I share my crazy God stories with? Who else knows my heart like you? Thank you for your hours of reading/editing and for your constant love and prayers. I pray that everyone who reads this book gets spiritual siblings like you, ones who "awaken the dawn" and who have fun nicknames like "Pitbull with lipstick"!

To my husband, Toby, and daughter, Gillian, thank you for your loving support behind the scenes. We may have a messy house, but we do not lack in love or in laughter. I am so thankful that we can be silly together.

To Dianne Salter, thank you for "encouraging" me to get out of my comfort zone. Sometimes we need to go kicking and screaming, to get where God wants us to be. I love you for that.

To Pam Williams, thank you for starting that writing group and for encouraging me to publish and blog.

To Aletha Baumgardner, thank you for being a part of the journey when it was getting hard to push through.

To Janice Riley and Marcy Rossi, thank you for being the final push that got this baby out! I appreciate your crash courses in self-publishing, editing, and marketing. You guys rock!

To Mom, Linda Horner, thank you for teaching me to pray to Jesus. That was my mustard seed of faith that grew.

And last, thank you Grandma, Mabel Pensinger, for giving me that Good News Bible when I was seven years old. I'm sorry I didn't open for another ten years, but when I did, that was the moment I knew God was real and my life changed forever. I can't wait to hug you again, in heaven.

Introduction

The Lord is speaking to you. Can you hear Him?

The Lord speaks to us in many ways: through His Word, through the still, small voice of the Holy Spirit, through other people, through dreams and visions, and even through nature. I know a young woman who hears from the Lord in songs and another who constantly sees numbers and dates the Lord uses to reveal meaning. For me, the Lord often gives images, pictures in my mind, when I am praying and meditating on His Word.

When God gives an image, I write it down in my journal. Each one is very special to me. One image might illustrate a verse I just read. Another might be the encouragement a friend needs that day. Some images hold deep revelation I return to over and over. Each one opens my heart to see Jesus, His character, and His Kingdom more vividly.

This devotional gives you an opportunity to connect with God for yourself through the *Sketch & Write* prompts. You don't need any special talents or skills. Give yourself permission and freedom to explore creativity with God. God is the Creator and we are made in His image, so He has given creativity to each one of us. Your sketches and writings are to be a conversation and expression with God. No one is going to see your work, except Him. And, if you get stuck, ask God what to draw, how to draw it, or what to write. He will answer you. It may come as an idea or a fleeting impression, or a color, or a song may come to mind…whatever comes, go with it! You can't get it wrong!

You can *Sketch & Write* in the space provided in the book or if you prefer, in your own journal. If your time is limited, I recommend you just read the devotion and come back to do the prompts. It's especially important to sit quietly and have alone time with the Lord, to seek Him as you respond to the prompts. It's okay to spend days on one devotion; you are nurturing intimacy with the Lord.

I pray you will be blessed by these devotions, and the Lord will take you deeper than you could ever imagine as you sketch and/or write each day. Let Him speak to you uniquely. Hearing the Lord becomes clearer as you get to know Him, just as you get to know a friend from talking and listening to them. Use your *Sketch & Write* time to imagine and meditate with God. He has so much He wants to share with you.

"He says, 'Be still, and know that I am God'..."
Psalm 46:10 NIV

Freedom to Express Yourself

What is this book? How do I use it?
What should I expect?

Often, we read books and then, we promptly forget what we read because there is no action or response. This book prompts you to take a step, one that partners with God to express yourself to Him.

My life began to change as I sought God. I read His Word, I journaled, and I prayed. Eventually, I began to be confident that I was hearing Him. Journaling became a major tool that assisted my spiritual growth. I journaled Scripture promises, quotes from Christian books, and important teachings. As I began to chronicle my conversations with God, He would sometimes continue them at later dates. I journaled dreams and visions, then I would ask God for their meanings. I would journal what He told me. Not only was I learning how to hear God for myself, I was learning more about who He was and how He created me.

This book shares images from my own devotional times with God - from my journals. The *Sketch & Write* prompts give you the opportunity to take action and to grow in new ways with God.

What is *Sketch & Write*? It's your creative response to what you read, meditate, and reflect on. Look at it as a conversation time with God. The prompts are there to assist you in engaging God creatively. Pick one or more of the prompts to do. You can do whatever you want in that space. You can doodle, or write a poem, or write what you hear God saying. Whatever you do, partner with God to do it. Let the Holy Spirit guide your time. Sit with God. Relax. Breathe. Be free to explore both sketching and writing.

Commit to reading this whole book and doing the *Sketch & Write* prompts. If you miss a day, pick it back up the next, but complete it. I promise it will challenge you. Some of the entries might offend you (to be honest, there have been things God showed me or told me that offended me, but His goal was to change or renew my mindset). You might not believe God showed me an image I share. That's okay. Test it. Take it to God. Ask Him. What does Scripture say? Or, is there something for you to learn?

Do not be conformed to this world, but be transformed by the renewal of your mind, that by testing you may discern what is the will of God, what is good and acceptable and perfect.
Romans 12:2 ESV

We each are uniquely made. We each can hear God. The Word says: My sheep hear my voice, and I know them, and they follow me (John 10:27 ESV). Hearing His voice comes as you get close to Jesus. It comes with intimacy. This devotional shares some of my most intimate moments with God and I believe that through them and the *Sketch & Write* prompts, you will encounter God and His heart. Be open and expectant.

My Definitions

Devotion – a set-aside time to focus whole-heartedly on God. A devotion or devotional is a tool to help you commune with God and to grow closer to Him.

Image – a visual in your mind or in the natural. An image might be a fleeting impression, a dream or vision, or something we see in creation that God wants to speak through. A Godly image will always reflect the true nature of God (love, peace, joy, hope, life, truth, goodness, righteousness, etc.).

Meditate – to think on and ponder, while asking God His perspective. Meditation is a form of prayer and is a partnership with the Holy Spirit to seek Godly revelation and understanding.

Hearing God – believing that God speaks and actively listening for Him. God may speak through a still, small voice, a thought, an image, through others, through nature, or even audibly. God can speak in many different ways and because He is a God of relationship, He wants us to hear Him and respond.

Sketch – creative expression through art. Sketching can include stick figures, doodles, cartoons, drawings, word art, coloring -- anything goes!

Write – creative expression through words. Writing can include journaling and poetry and capture thoughts and memories, impressions, experiences, and conversations with God. Writing also helps us remember what God has done. We can go back to read and remember.

- Day 1 -

IMAGE: STAMPS OF APPROVAL

Submit yourselves therefore to God.
James 4:7 KJV

As I was reading James 4:7, I wanted to do just what it said. I wanted to submit myself to God, so I imagined myself under His authority. After a moment there, I sensed the Lord stamping "approved" seals all over me, like little ink stamps on my skin; on my arms, on my hands, and one on each of my fingers. They reminded me of stamps like those used to re-enter amusement parks, but these were tiny marks of approval from the Father, each stamp speaking to me, "I love you. I approve of you. You are Mine… ." As I assessed my ink-kissed skin, I thought, *Who can come against what the Lord approves of?*

> *What, then, shall we say in response to these things?*
> *If God is for us, who can be against us?*
> Romans 8:31 NIV

PROMPTS:

Imagine God's stamp of approval on you.
What does it look like? Draw it.

Meditate with God on today's verses or image.
Write what you hear.

_____

_____

_____

_____

_____

_____

_____

_____

_____

_____

- Day 2 -

IMAGE: RECORDING WITH DELIGHT

"The LORD your God is in your midst,
...He will exult over you with joy, He will be quiet in
His love. He will rejoice over you..."
Zephaniah 3:17 AMP

As I was praying, I was taken into the Heavenly Father's presence. I wanted His attention, but I noticed He was working. I sat near Him to wait. As I did, I watched Him write in a book. He stopped to mark something on a board. Then He wrote in the book again. He stopped and marked on the board. This went on for a while. I wondered, "What is He writing? What is He marking?" When He finished, I asked Him these questions.

Smiling, He replied, "I am writing about My children, and I pause to mark when one comes to know Me, through My Son, Jesus." I sensed, by the Spirit, He keeps a record of all this with great joy and delight!

Then those who feared the LORD talked with each other, and the
LORD listened and heard. A scroll of remembrance was written in
his presence concerning those who feared the
LORD and honored his name.
Malachi 3:16 NIV

PROMPTS:

Meditate on today's verses. Allow the Father's love to envelop you and then respond. Draw or Write.

What date did God record for your salvation? Ask Father God for His perspective of the memory. What does He want to tell you about the experience?

_____

_____

_____

_____

_____

_____

Extra: As far back as I remember, I believed in Jesus, but I didn't have a specific date for my salvation. I often wondered about this, so I asked the Lord if I had one. He reminded me of the time when I was seventeen years old, and I was sobbing over a breakup. For some reason, I opened up the unused Bible my grandmother had given me, to Psalms. When I began reading, I physically experienced the peace that passes all understanding. My crying stopped abruptly, and I sat amazed, wondering how a book could do that. God told me that was the moment I knew He was real. That was my salvation date; The day I believed.

- Day 3 -

IMAGE: CREATIVITY CLASS

In the beginning God created the heavens and the earth. Now the earth was formless and empty, darkness was over the surface of the deep, and the Spirit of God was hovering over the waters.
Genesis 1:1-2 NIV

I had a dream I was in a large art classroom; the subject was Creativity Class. The teacher gave us three assignments. First assignment: Take a long black piece of felt and poke holes in it to create designs, so light will shine through once displayed. Second assignment: Design and make a hot-air balloon and fly it. Part of the assignment explanation included going outside to see another class already testing their creations. The sky was full of unique hot-air balloons and baskets. Third assignment: We would each be given an empty wardrobe - we were to create and build three different features on the inside. The features could be functional (like shelves or drawers), or more artistic and whimsical.

He has filled them with skill to do all kinds of work as engravers, designers, embroiderers in blue, purple and scarlet yarn and fine linen, and weavers—all of them skilled workers and designers.
Exodus 35:35 NIV

- Sketch & Write -

PROMPTS:

Today's devotion is about releasing the creativity that God placed in you. So have fun with God. If you get stuck, ask Him what He wants you to draw or write. Choose one of the assignments from today's devotion (or create your own) and draw your design.

Meditate on Exodus 35:35.
What is God calling you to create or do?

_____

_____

_____

_____

_____

_____

_____

Extra: "But, I'm not creative!" -- If that's your response to today's prompts, think on this: God, The Creator, lives in you and therefore, so does creativity. Ask Him to create through you. It might not be art. It might be a solution to a community need that you have the skill or ability to meet. Creativity can include ideas, solutions, and problem-solving.

- *Day* 4 -

IMAGE: THE GAMBLER

emmanne

While Jesus was having dinner at Levi's house, many tax collectors
and sinners were eating with him and his disciples,
for there were many who followed him.
Mark 2:15 NIV

I was praying - focusing on God and worshipping Him - when I saw
an image in my mind of a thin man with long hair, who was dressed
like a slick gambler. His eyes twinkled as he smiled at me. Then I
recognized Him. It was Jesus! I was shocked. I did not expect Him to
be dressed like that. He asked me, "Why am I dressed like a
gambler?"

I was thinking on it, when He knelt beside me and answered his own
question: "I like gamblers. I hang out with them. Liars, cheats, prosti-
tutes -- Give Me the worst and see what I can do. No case is too hard
for Me."

...they asked... "Why does he eat with tax collectors and sinners?"
On hearing this, Jesus said to them, "It is not the healthy
who need a doctor, but the sick. I have not come
to call the righteous, but sinners."
Mark 2:16-17 NIV

PROMPTS:

Draw or doodle about your transformation in Christ Jesus,
from sinner to saint.

Write about a time when God did something that you did not expect.

Remember a time when you were hard to love.
Trace the journey with Jesus you are on and take encouragement at
the changes and mile markers.

_____

_____

_____

_____

_____

_____

_____

_____

_____

_____

- Day 5 -

IMAGE: WOUNDED HEART

He heals the brokenhearted and binds up their wounds.
Psalm 147:3 NIV

I was praying for someone who had hurt me, and God showed me an image of her heart. One section of the heart had built-up crusty layers over an original wound. It wasn't just unpleasant to look at, it was repulsive. The hard layers were intended to protect the heart, but instead, over time, they repelled anyone who tried to get close to the person.

I asked God to tenderly remove each layer of scar tissue and to heal her heart completely so that the heart would be softened and able to love.

I will give you a new heart and put a new spirit in you; I will remove from you your heart of stone and give you a heart of flesh.
Ezekiel 36:26 NIV

PROMPTS:

Examine your own heart with Jesus. Draw your heart, wounds, and all.

Then, draw it, according to Ezekiel 36:26, new, in Christ Jesus.

Ask Jesus, "What do You want to do with my heart right now?" What hurt(s) come to mind? Write them down as you talk to Jesus and allow Him to heal your heart.

_____

_____

_____

_____

_____

_____

Extra: Coming to the place where you can pray for someone who has hurt you, takes forgiveness, with Jesus' help. It's a process. I had months, even years, of bringing hurts to Jesus, giving them up (not holding on to them), and allowing Jesus to heal me. Eventually, I was able to pray for the person, so that they can experience heart healing, just as I had, through Christ.

- Day 6 -

IMAGE: BULLDOZING THE GLORY

"All the glory You have given to Me, I pass on to them. May that glory unify them and make them one as We are one, I in them and You in Me, that they may be refined so that all will know that You sent Me, and You love them in the same way You love Me."
John 17:22-23 VOICE

I was sitting with the Lord, crying because I felt so broken and needy, having fallen short again. Then, the Lord gave me an image of myself on the Father's lap. The image changed and I was being heaped up like sand. God was bulldozing me and millions of other people into dunes. I realized we were not grains of sand at all. We were grains of glory that God was heaping up together to be stored and later released. I thought, "We, His glory?!"

Then God showed me Matthew 6:19-21 AMP.
"Do not store up for yourselves [material] treasures on earth, where moth and rust destroy, and where thieves break in and steal. But store up for yourselves treasures in heaven, where neither moth nor rust destroys, and where thieves do not break in and steal; for where your treasure is, there your heart [your wishes, your desires; that on which your life centers] will be also."

The Lord also does what He tells us to do in this passage. He stores us up together, for we were meant for unity with Him and with each other. The Lord also does what He tells us to do in this passage. He stores us up together, for we were meant for unity with Him and with each other. He values us like treasure. He puts His Spirit, His glory in us and we are His inheritance, and we are where His heart is. I am undone by this revelation.

God [in His eternal plan] chose to make known to them how great for the Gentiles are the riches of the glory of this mystery, which is Christ in and among you, the hope and guarantee of [realizing the] glory.
Colossians 1:27 AMP

Sketch & Write

PROMPTS:

What is glory? How can we be glory?
Meditate, research, and write about glory.

What does glory look like? Sound like? Feel like?
Does it have weight? Draw it.

_____

_____

_____

_____

_____

_____

_____

_____

_____

_____

- Day 7 -

IMAGE: FAMILY HUG

*Therefore, since we are surrounded by such a
great cloud of witnesses...*
Hebrews 12:1 NIV

I awoke and sensed I was being hugged by the Trinity (Father, Son, and Holy Spirit) and around them, the angels and saints wanted to hug me too and they all crowded in. It was wonderful – a huge spiritual bear hug, so full and enveloping! And the best part was the revelation: this was *my family*.

I belonged and was accepted *whole-heartedly.*

This spiritual family hug deeply touched my heart - because I can't imagine my earthly, natural extended family ever doing that, due to brokenness, strife, and distance. I am so thankful God gives us a new family in Christ Jesus, who is good and loving.

God sets the lonely in families...
Psalm 68:6 NIV

PROMPTS:

Draw (even if just stick figures) the family hug in today's devotion.
Put yourself in the middle, surrounded by your spiritual family.
Allow yourself to be flooded with their love.

What do you need from your family (love, acceptance, etc.)?
Write those needs out and ask Jesus to provide them.

_____

_____

_____

_____

_____

_____

_____

_____

_____

- *Day 8* -

IMAGE: FOLLOW HIS FEET

emShine

Ah, how beautiful the feet of those on the mountain who declare the
good news of victory, of peace and liberation…
Isaiah 52:7 VOICE

I woke one morning to the image of the Lord's feet. They were
massive in size and they were walking. First, His feet walked inside
on tiled floors. Then, they moved outside to sandy soil, then to rocky
mountain ground, and finally, His feet began running on water. I saw
only His feet.

We are to follow Jesus' feet, wherever they go. His powerful steps
will guide us. No matter the terrain, it's easy - all we have to do is
follow.

…He said to him, "Follow Me." And he left everything behind,
and got up and began to follow Him.
Luke 5:27-28 AMP

- Sketch & Write -

PROMPTS:

Draw Jesus' feet or sandal prints on the page.
Dream and pray, and commit to follow Him.

Meditate on Jesus' feet. How do you see them stepping?
How big are they? What do you see them taking you into?
Where are you willing to follow Him to? Write.

_____

_____

_____

_____

_____

_____

_____

_____

_____

_____

_____

- Day 9 -

IMAGE: LIGHT IN THE DARK

emmanuel

The LORD is with me; I will not be afraid.
What can mere mortals do to me?
Psalm 118:6 NIV

I bowed before God and praised Him. In a vision, I saw myself in a dark, grimy room with little light. There was a small table in the middle of the room, and I stood beside it. God asked, "Where is the light coming from?" I looked around and realized that it was coming from inside me. This light was the only light in the room.

I began to sing praises and gave thanks to God. I laughed out loud because God was renewing me, healing me of all my wounds. Nothing whatsoever could hurt me. No one could kill me, for this Light was eternal. I laughed with pure joy! Though my body (flesh) may die, my spirit lives forever and I am with My Father always. How glorious! Jesus' light and love fill me and shine out of me continuously. I can sing and praise Him despite dire-looking circumstances.

After they had been severely flogged, they were thrown into prison...
About midnight Paul and Silas were praying
and singing hymns to God...
Acts 16:23-25 NIV

PROMPTS:

Draw yourself with God's light shining from within.
How does the light extend out? In what ways?

Think of a time when there was light in the dark for you.
Perhaps you couldn't see but one step at a time,
but God was leading you.
Write about it.

_____

_____

_____

_____

_____

_____

_____

_____

_____

- Day 10 -

IMAGE: LIT-UP GRAPES

For you were once darkness, but now you are light in the Lord.
Live as children of light (for the fruit of the light
consists in all goodness, righteousness and truth).
Ephesians 5: 8-19 NIV

I had a dream where I saw clusters of grapes. Some clusters were lit up on the inside. I picked those. The light was life (eternal). These were not normal, natural grapes. They were supernatural.

As I reflect on this dream, I realize the lit-up grapes represent born-again believers. They look like normal people on the outside, but they actually are lit up on the inside with the light of the world, Jesus. They are a new creation and completely different from the way they used to be. Now, they shine for Jesus to show those in darkness the way, the truth, and the life.

I have been crucified with Christ and I no longer live,
but Christ lives in me...
Galatians 2:20 NIV

PROMPTS:

Draw clusters of grapes. Color some dark and some light.
Associate people's names with both types of grapes.
Which name does God highlight to you?
Reach out to that person this week.

Who do you know that is a lit-up grape?
How do you see their light in how they live? Write.

_____

_____

_____

_____

_____

_____

_____

_____

_____

_____

- Day 11 -

IMAGE: RESTLESS HAND SYNDROME

emSzune

"I have the right to do anything," you say—but not everything is beneficial. "I have the right to do anything"
—but not everything is constructive.
1 Corinthians 10:23 NIV

I was praying with two friends, and I sensed a deep peace and rest come. Then, God showed me a hand holding an object. The hand constantly checked the item, feeling it and fiddling with it. The hand was never at rest. As with an addiction, it was unable to stop moving.

I believe God was showing me a major problem with man today – we are unable to put things down. If we would put them down, we would experience the peace and rest we so deeply need.

"Come to me, all you who are weary and burdened, and I will give you rest. Take my yoke upon you and learn from me, for I am gentle and humble in heart, and you will find rest for your souls. For my yoke is easy and my burden is light."
Matthew 11:28-30 NIV

PROMPTS:

In today's image, what do you see the hand holding? Draw or write.

Personally, what do you need to put down (social media, worry, unforgiveness, regret, selfishness, busyness, etc.)? Write out a prayer and release that thing to God. Invite in Jesus' peace and rest.

_____

_____

_____

_____

_____

_____

_____

_____

_____

- Day 12 -

IMAGE: BEAUTIFYING HIS BEARD

"As I looked, "thrones were set in place, and the Ancient of Days took his seat. His clothing was as white as snow; the hair of his head was white like wool…"
Daniel 7:9 NIV

While worshipping the Lord I had an image of myself, in the Spirit, making Hawaiian-like white leis that hung straight down. I was entwining white flowers on long white strands. My view zoomed out, and I saw that the strands were actually hairs in a long, flowing beard. Then, revelation overwhelmed me as I realized the beard belonged to God the Father! In my worship, He was allowing me to beautify His beard.

The moment was so beautiful, so holy, so intimate. God showed me through this image, that my act of worship was an act of love from a child to her father. I didn't know that my song and praise was being transformed into a gift of adornment highly valued by my Father.

Give to the Lord the glory he deserves! Bring your offering and come into his presence. Worship the Lord in all his holy splendor.
1 Chronicles 16:29 NLT

PROMPTS:

Worship and praise the Lord with your drawings and words.
Beautify the page for Him.

Put on worship music and sit with God.
Ask Him what gift of love He would like today.

_____

_____

_____

_____

_____

_____

_____

_____

_____

- Day 13 -

IMAGE: SKYDIVING DOG (PART I: LOYAL)

"I no longer call you servants, because a servant does not know his master's business. Instead, I have called you friends, for everything that I learned from my Father I have made known to you."
John 15:15 NIV

I took a walk on my lunch break. It was a beautiful day with many puffy clouds in the sky. When I looked up, I saw a cloud shaped like a skydiving dog, with legs stretched out wide. Two words immediately came to mind: "Loyal" and "Freedom," and the Holy Spirit said to me, "Those who are <u>loyal</u> to Me experience more and more freedom." Then, He said, "Describe a loyal dog."

My response - A loyal dog obeys and trusts his master, lays down his life for him, is at his feet, is by his side, follows him, relies on him for food and care, and delights to be with him. The dog also brings comfort and companionship to his master. The relationship is not one-sided. I realized this is how it is with us. We are not dogs, by any means, but the loyal dog image depicts our relationship with God. When we are true followers of Jesus, we move from a master-servant relationship to a loyal friend and companion of God, who can be trusted with the work of the Kingdom.

...Jesus asked Simon Peter, "...do you love Me?"
Jesus said, "Then feed my sheep."
John 21:15-17 NLT

PROMPTS:

Draw a loyal dog or a skydiving dog.
What is speaking to you through the image?

Meditate on the word "*loyalty*." Invite God to speak to you about this word. What comes to mind? How has God been loyal to you? How would you like to be more loyal to Him? Write and pray.

_____

_____

_____

_____

_____

_____

_____

_____

_____

- Day 14 -

IMAGE: SKYDIVING DOG (PART II: FREEDOM)

emShnne

So think of it this way: if the Son comes to make you free,
you will really be free.
John 8:36 VOICE

Freedom. God gave me this word when He showed me the image of the skydiving dog in the clouds. He said, "Those who are loyal to Me experience more and more freedom," so I wanted to dig deeper into this revelation. I closed my eyes and waited on the Holy Spirit.

After a moment I heard His still, small voice say, "When I set someone free, they are free indeed. There is no shame or debris left. Like a prisoner being released after years in a dark cell, he steps into bright light and smells freedom in the air. I bought you for a high price and freedom was completely paid for. Stretch out your arms. Open up your hands, let go of all the things from your slavery days, and fly. You are free to seek Me, free to dance and worship Me, free to come close to hear My secrets, and free to do My Kingdom work. Freedom in Me is the best; it's the highest rush you will ever experience. Come skydive with Me."

It is for freedom that Christ has set us free. Stand firm, then, and do
not let yourselves be burdened again by a yoke of slavery.
Galatians 5:1 NIV

PROMPTS:

Have you ever been skydiving or ever dreamed of flying?
Draw or write.

Meditate on the word "*Freedom*." Read this devotion again, but read
it aloud and allow the words to speak directly to you. Allow God's
freedom to envelop you and let go of any burdens. Write.

_____

_____

_____

_____

_____

_____

_____

_____

_____

_____

- *Day 15* -

IMAGE: COMPOST

*You were dead because of your sins and because
your sinful nature was not yet cut away. Then God
made you alive with Christ, for He forgave all our sins.*
Colossians 2:13 NLT

Just before sleep came, the Lord showed me a forest, but I could only
see a small sliver of it. By a tree, ferns, mushrooms, and moss grew
out of a bed of dead leaves and twigs in various states of decompo-
sition. In this vision, I could even smell the earthiness of it. Then, the
Holy Spirit said, "From years of decay came nutrient-rich soil."

I am the tree in the forest. I think back on my life, on the things that
didn't go as planned. Sin, heartaches, disappointments—the stuff of
life in a fallen world—are all littered around me. I've learned from
them. I've grown because of them. I am made strong because of the
nutrients from their compost. Jesus takes dead, decaying things and
makes life spring up.

*...to comfort all who mourn, and provide for those who grieve in Zion
— to bestow on them a crown of beauty instead of ashes, the oil of
joy instead of mourning, and a garment of praise instead of a
spirit of despair. They will be called oaks of righteousness,
a planting of the LORD for the display of his splendor.*
Isaiah 61:2-3 NIV

PROMPTS:

What decaying things litter, or have littered, your life? Draw yourself as a tree and write those things at the base of the tree. Picture Jesus turning them into nutrient-rich soil, and then draw plants growing up from them. What good thing does each plant represent?

Reflect back on your life. How has Jesus redeemed dead things and brought new life to you? Write.

_____

_____

_____

_____

_____

_____

_____

_____

Extra: Some examples of decaying things might be loneliness, broken relationships, illness, pain, loss, fear, hurt, trauma, and sin.

- Day 16 -

IMAGE: SACK OF GLORY

I pray that the eyes of your heart may be enlightened in order that you may know the hope to which he has called you, the riches of his glorious inheritance in his holy people…
Ephesians 1:18 NIV

I was sitting with the Lord, and He said, "I'm going to drop something into your spirit." I sensed that it was big, so I prepared to receive it by opening myself up like a hatch on a submarine. In the Spirit, God released an enormous sack. Its heavy weight hit my spirit-well with a huge splash and sank fast, going down, down, down. In the vision, I was now swimming, so I kicked to the well's bottom to see it better. The sack was much bigger than me and was covered in a canvas-like material, but I saw no zipper or opening, nor any markings.

I asked, "Lord, what is it? Why did you give it to me?" He urged me to look inside. So, I went in by faith and it was filled with glory, the heavy weight of a substance unseen. To my flesh, the inside was empty, but to my spirit, it was full—the hope of glory. The Lord said, "I have deposited a taste of the hope of glory into your spirit for you to *see*, to *imagine*, to *experience* and to *interact* with. Explore it further."

May He grant you out of the riches of His glory, to be strengthened and spiritually energized with power through His Spirit in your inner self, [indwelling your innermost being and personality]...
Ephesians 3:16 AMP

PROMPTS:

What does God want to drop into your spirit today?
Imagine with Him. Draw or write.

Explore *glory* for yourself. Use all your senses to explore this
unseen substance. Draw or write.

_____

_____

_____

_____

_____

_____

_____

_____

_____

_____

_____

- Day 17 -

IMAGE: NEW TOOLSET

*"But seek first the kingdom of God and his righteousness,
and all these things will be added to you."*
Matthew 6:33 NIV

I got up early to spend time with the Lord. As I was talking with Him, I sensed two angels to my left. I welcomed them. They knelt down and held out their hands. In their hands were tools. I asked the Lord what to do. He said, "Take them." So, by faith, I took the tools and put them in my heart. Then I thanked the angels and asked the Lord for the purpose of the tools.

Jesus replied, "To help you. You need new tools at this stage of your growth. I give you exactly what you need, when you need it. This is a new toolset. It comes with promotion, a new job. These two angels also are provided to help you. They know the tools and the work. They are experienced professionals to mentor you. They bless you in your work. They honor you and are grateful to be a part of your team."

And my God will supply every need of yours...
Philippians 4:19 NIV

PROMPTS:

If the Lord was giving you a new toolset, what tools would be
included? Imagine with the Lord. What do the tools look like?
What do they do? Draw or write about them.

Is there a time when God gave you just what you needed,
when you needed it? Write.

_____

_____

_____

_____

_____

_____

_____

*Extra: Shortly after this encounter with God, my husband and I
sensed that it was time to find a new church home. When we found
one, I wondered where I would fit in. My past ministry work didn't fit
at the new church. Then, one Sunday, during a sermon, I felt the call
to join the Prayer Team. As I look back, I believe that the new toolset
was for this ministry, to pray for all God wants to accomplish in and
through this body of believers.*

- Day 18 -

IMAGE: STAINED GLASS CROWN

You will be a crown of splendor in the LORD's hand,
a royal diadem in the hand of your God.
Isaiah 62:3 NIV

I was just about to fall asleep when I saw an image of a huge tree. Its canopy was filled with colors, even blues, reds and purples. From my vantage point on the ground, it was like a glorious stained-glass crown.

This image spurred me to meditate on the word *crown*, which is a symbol of nobility, authority, and victory, and then specifically on my own personal crown. What does my crown look like? What is it made of? Spiritually, what does it represent? From Scripture, we know we can be given a crown of life (James 1:12), a crown of righteousness (2 Timothy 4:8), and a crown of glory (1 Peter 5:4).

I heard the Lord say to me, "Those who are in Me, do indeed receive a crown. When you set your mind on things above, you come into a kingdom mindset. I am the King *of Kings* and Lord *of Lords*. I desire for My children to become kings and lords and when they do, I crown them with My attributes."

Surrounding the throne were twenty-four other thrones, and seated on them were twenty-four elders. They were dressed in white and had crowns of gold on their heads.
Revelation 4:4 NIV

PROMPTS:

With God, visualize your own personal crown. What is it made of?
Does it have a design or words on it? Does it have stones or gems?
Colors? Ask God what each aspect means? Draw or write.

Imagine yourself receiving your crown from Jesus. Allow Him to
place it on your head. What are you thinking and feeling? Write this
out in conversation to the Lord.

_____

_____

_____

_____

_____

_____

_____

_____

_____

- Day 19 -

IMAGE: AN ARROW WITH ROOTS

*Even then, God was preparing my mouth to speak
like a sharp sword...He crafted me into a sharp-tipped arrow and
tucked me away in His quiver...*
Isaiah 49:2 VOICE

I was listening to soaking worship music as I re-read an old journal. I closed my eyes and contemplated some of the promises God had given me. In the Spirit, I saw an angel give me an arrow. The head was made of flint, but the tail was not what I was expecting. Instead of ending with a fletching of feathers, the shaft had grown tree-like roots.

Immediately, I knew what the Holy Spirit was saying to me – I was a planting of the Lord. My roots were in Him, and I was called to be shared with others. I was to be a living arrow shooting into the world. These words hit my spirit: "surety," "straightness," "hitting the target," and "the Lord does not miss."

I heard, "You are Mine, firmly rooted in Me. I am pruning you and you are growing in knowledge and understanding. You are being strengthened. Continue to stand in Me. Do not back down. Be ready for every opportunity. They are precious, not only for others, but for you. Be ready to move as I direct."

*...they will grow like a cedar of Lebanon; planted in the house of
the Lord, ...They will still bear fruit in old age, they will stay fresh and
green, proclaiming, 'The Lord is upright....'*
Psalm 92:12-15 NIV

– Sketch & Write –

PROMPTS:

Draw an arrow with roots.
What is God saying to *you* through this image?

Where is your arrow headed? Talk to God about His plans for you
and write down what you hear.

Where are your roots planted? Reflect on your spiritual history,
family heritage, and/or the body of believers you are with. How do
they affect you and help you to grow?

_____

_____

_____

_____

_____

_____

Extra: My "spiritual roots" - My grandmother had strong faith and she prayed for me. My mother taught me how to pray to Jesus. My church family encouraged me and sharpened me. Also, my own seeking of God has grown my roots. All these have helped me to be firmly planted in Christ Jesus.

- Day 20 -

IMAGE: THE BURN

Grace be with all who love our
Lord Jesus Christ with undying and incorruptible love.
Ephesians 6:24 AMP

While worshipping with other believers and in the Spirit, I saw the beginning of a forest fire. It started at the edge of some woods and was not a full blaze yet. I heard God say, "*You don't know how to fully burn yet.* You have a measure of burn and in time you will burn more fully and you will ignite others. Come into My consuming fire. Dwell there, till it burns up all the dross, till you are purified like gold, radiant and shining."

As I meditated on this, I remembered times of sitting out under the stars, watching the slow burn of a campfire, mesmerized by the flickering light and glowing embers. The ***burn*** is an invitation of intimacy with God. I think of God's consuming fire and imagine it, not as a hot, fiery furnace, but as a slow-burning campfire where I am nestled inside and where God tenderly purifies me with His caressing flames of love.

And he shall sit as a refiner and purifier of silver: and he shall purify
the sons of Levi, and purge them as gold and silver, that they may
offer unto the Lord *an offering in righteousness.*
Malachi 3:3 KJV

— Sketch & Write —

PROMPTS:

Meditate with God on one of these words: burn, love,
consuming fire, or purify. Write.

If you were to accept the invitation to *burn* with God,
what would that look like? Draw or write.

_____

_____

_____

_____

_____

_____

_____

_____

_____

_____

*Extra: I often join a gathering called The Burn where there is no
agenda, only a desire to worship God wholeheartedly. Some sing,
some play instruments, some dance - all are beautiful expressions
and offerings of love to God.*

- *Day 21* -

IMAGE: HIDDEN UNDER HIM

He will cover you with his feathers. He will shelter you with his wings. His faithful promises are your armor and protection.
Psalm 91:4 NLT

While focusing on God, I saw myself at the Father's feet. I climbed in under His throne. Under Him, I curled up in a ball, in His shelter, while His cascading robe fell all around me. I thought, *He is my refuge and my security*. I was being hidden in the cleft of the Rock and under the shadow of His wings. It was a good place and I didn't ever want to leave.

The cares of this world seemed so small at this vantage point, so close to My God. Underneath His protection, I did not have to be afraid. I did not have to worry about my latest mistake or my latest regret. I could just rest in His presence and be assured that I was safe and sound.

> *"...and while My glory is passing by, I will put you in a cleft of the rock and protectively cover you with My hand until I have passed by."*
> Exodus 33:22 AMP

— Sketch & Write —

PROMPTS:

Where (or Who) is your hiding place? Why? Draw or write.

What do you need from God right now? Write Him a letter.
Be expectant that He will meet your need.

Meditate on today's Scriptures. What speaks to you most?
Draw or write.

_____

_____

_____

_____

_____

_____

_____

_____

_____

_____

- *Day 22* -

IMAGE: BUILDING INFRASTRUCTURE

*You are being built on a solid foundation… with Jesus,
the Anointed Himself, the precious cornerstone. The building is
joined together stone by stone—all of us chosen and sealed in
Him, rising up to become a holy temple in the Lord.*
Ephesians 2:20-22 VOICE

I woke up knowing I had just been dreaming, but I could not remember the dream. The only thing that came to me were these words: **Go back a page or two and see the infrastructure He's building**. I knew it was a call to remember what God had been doing in my life.

Memories of how God had touched me over the years began to flood my mind. Each one built faith and belief in who He is and who I am, in Him. From my encounter with God in the Psalms at age seventeen to being filled with the Holy Spirit in my forties, He has been teaching me how to worship, how to spend time with Him, how to be obedient, how to be generous, how to surrender, and how to love. I have so far to go, but I see I have made some progress. I know His work is *good* and He is building something amazing!

*As you come to him, the living Stone—rejected by humans but chosen
by God and precious to him— you also, like living stones, are being
built into a spiritual house to be a holy priesthood…*
1 Peter 2:4-5 NIV

PROMPTS:

Picture yourself as a building. What part of the construction is God working on right now? Draw.

Think back over the years and recall pivotal moments in your Christian journey. Write or do a timeline.

_____

_____

_____

_____

_____

_____

_____

_____

_____

_____

_____

_____

- Day 23 -

IMAGE: INNER WELL

emmanuel

With joy you will draw water from the wells of salvation.
Isaiah 12:3 VOICE

At the evening worship service, someone began to play the saxophone from somewhere in the back of the room. The music was unlike anything I'd heard before. It began like light dancing over me. Notes of purity and comfort flowed in the air and surrounded me like heavenly wings. The room fell away, and I was alone with the Lord. The music sang to me; I somehow knew that healing and restoration was happening in deep places within me.

The sounds were like drops of rain in my spirit. They fell upon the dry places in my being I didn't even know existed. They fell into a deep well inside of me. The quiet, gentle drops splashed one by one. As they hit the water, my spirit began to move with the rippling waves. I opened myself to accept the replenishment and the water began to flow. Piano notes then mixed with the saxophone, and the water fell at a faster rate into my inner wellspring. As my spirit was being nourished with Living Water, tears flowed down my cheeks in thanksgiving to the Giver. I was overwhelmed by God's goodness.

"I offer water that will become a wellspring within you that gives life throughout eternity. You will never be thirsty again."
John 4:14 VOICE

PROMPTS:

What type of music ministers to you? Play something and ask the Lord to meet you in it. Draw or write about how the music touches you or what God is speaking to you through it.

Meditate on John 4:14. Are you spiritually dry? Ask to be filled with Living Water. Draw or write.

_____

_____

_____

_____

_____

_____

_____

Extra: During the time that the saxophonist ministered to us, I also felt the Lord honoring the gifts and talents of the people who sacrifice daily to be the hands and feet of Jesus. The musical notes seemed to sing, "I honor you". It made me so thankful to the musicians and ministers. How can we bless those in ministry who give so much?

- Day 24 -

IMAGE: HIGHWAY OF PRAISE

*Sing to God, sing praises to His name, cast up a highway for Him
Who rides through the deserts—His name is the Lord—
be in high spirits and glory before Him!*
Psalm 68:4 AMPC

An unexpected phenomenon occurred as I was listening to an audio
CD on my DVD player for the first time. Instead of video, the DVD
player displayed a visual of the sound waves of the Christian teacher
I was listening to. His voice patterns first formed circles, which
changed to form hills. Then, they changed again to form a path
between two mountains. That's when my eyes grew wide in wonder;
That was the moment when Psalm 68:4 came alive to me. I was
watching words create a highway.

I had been captivated for years by this verse in Psalm 68, but
perplexed at how praises could cast up a highway, but the DVD
visual showed me how it works. Just as God spoke the universe into
existence, our words and praises have the power to create too. As we
praise God, it forms a highway for Him. He sits enthroned on our
praises and He rides on them. Our praises actually ***move*** Him!

Yet you are holy, enthroned on the praises of Israel.
Psalm 22:3 NLT

PROMPTS:

Fill the page with praises to God. Speak them aloud and cast up a highway for God to ride on.

In the devotion today, sound waves created circles, hills, mountains, and paths. If praises created colorful drawings, what would they look like? Pick a praise word (e.g., hallelujah, glory, magnify, exalt, adore) and draw it in praise of God.

_____

_____

_____

_____

_____

_____

_____

Extra: If our praises build roads for God to move on, would the opposite also be true? Would grumbling and complaining tear roads down? Would the lack of praises mean no highways and no moves of God?

- *Day* 25 -

IMAGE: NARROW BEACH TRAIL

"Enter through the narrow gate. For wide is the gate and broad is the road that leads to destruction, and many enter through it. But small is the gate and narrow the road that leads to life, and only a few find it."
Matthew 7:13-14 NIV

I was in worship when I saw an image of a very narrow beach trail almost hidden by brush. The trail was one-foot-in-front-of-the-other wide. It was Jesus' path, so narrow, most miss it when taking in the vast landscape. Jesus said to me, "Are you willing to travel it? If so, I will lead you, even by the hand." At my nod, He tenderly reached for my arm and guided me into the tight opening. We went over dunes and across driftwood. As we walked, I realized that His guidance was a very precious thing. It was a special and sacred commitment for Him; a promise to never leave me, nor forsake me.

Time passed to late evening and the path opened to the beach. Here, the moonlight reflected off of the glassy-black ocean and the stark contrast caused me to ponder an even greater disparity. Here was Jesus, the Light of the world and He was standing next to me, one who used to be black with sin. Now redeemed, I could reflect His light as I followed Him on the narrow trail, the Way of Life.

"The LORD himself goes before you and will be with you; he will never leave you nor forsake you..."
Deuteronomy 31:8 NIV

PROMPTS:

Imagine you are walking behind Jesus on His narrow path. Where does He take you? What does He say? What does He point out to you? Draw or write about the experience.

Meditate on today's Scriptures and open a conversation with God. What do you want to ask Him? You can ask hard questions. Then, listen for His answers and write what you hear.

_____

_____

_____

_____

_____

_____

Extra: Hearing God can come in different ways. Once, I asked God where He had been during a turbulent time in my life. His answer came as a memory. I remembered how a family took me in so that I could finish college when my first marriage failed. I realized that God had been there, that He had provided for me, and I hadn't known it at the time!

- Day 26 -

IMAGE: SEISMIC AUDIO ARRAY SPEAKER

*And he gave the apostles, the prophets, the evangelists, the shepherds
and teachers, to equip the saints for the work of ministry,
for building up the body of Christ.*
Ephesians 4:11-12 ESV

I watched the movie "I Can Only Imagine" before going to bed.
Before I fell asleep, I had a vision. I was among black boxes in low
lighting. I was backstage in a theater venue, and the boxes were
music equipment. Surprisingly, I realized I was not a person; I was
one of the black boxes. I was then moved onto the stage and plugged
in. I then knew I was a speaker! The plug and cord were my
connection to power (to God; to Holy Spirit). I spoke only what God
told me to say. I was humbled and honored to be a ***speaker*** (an
instrument) for Him.

After the vision was over, I got up and looked up speakers on the
internet, trying to find one that looked like the one in my vision. The
Seismic Audio Compact 2x5 Line Array Speaker with Titanium
Compression Driver for $279.99 appeared the closest. I laughed out
loud at the long-winded product name and thanked God for His
humor, and for the unique way He confirmed my calling.

*For we are God's handiwork, created in Christ Jesus to do good
works, which God prepared in advance for us to do.*
Ephesians 2:10 NIV

PROMPTS:

In today's devotion, God used an unusual image, a sound speaker, to confirm purpose and calling. Sit with God and explore how He uniquely made you. Ask Him to show you an object, animal, or plant that speaks to your purpose. Ask Him many questions about what He shows you. Draw or write.

Re-read Ephesians 4:11-12. Do you know which role God is calling you to? Look at your life. What clues do you see? Pray and seek God's will for your life.

_____

_____

_____

_____

_____

_____

_____

- Day 27 -

IMAGE: PIPE WITH LIQUID GOLD

...I will pour out my spirit upon all flesh...
Joel 2:28 KJV

During worship at a gathering, I saw (in the spirit realm) a pipe near the top of the wall. Out of it came a thick golden substance, flowing like honey, and somehow, I knew that it was **purity**. My intellect tried to grasp this spiritual image, but my heart was so hungry for the Lord, that if it was from Him, I wanted it! In faith, I stood under its flow; it poured over and covered me completely.

I heard the Lord say, "I pour out My gold on you. From My temple to you, a royal priest and king, I cover you in My glory. You carry My presence. Let this reality expand in you. My radiance, like pure gold, shines from you and is seen by others. It is very appealing and desirable. Your seeking of Me affects others." Then He asks, "Why did you go under the flow of liquid gold?"

I answered, "To be more in You, O Lord. I just want more of You."

I counsel you to buy from me gold refined by fire, so that you may be rich, and white garments so that you may clothe yourself..., and salve to anoint your eyes, so that you may see.
Revelation 3:18 ESV

PROMPTS:

Meditate on spiritual purity. Have an open conversation with God. What does it mean to be purified or refined? What is He speaking to your heart about purity? Write.

Meditate on Revelation 3:18. Focus on one of these from the verse: gold, white garments, or salve. Which speaks to you right now? Why? Draw or write.

Extra: Spiritual encounters with the Lord can be out of the ordinary, but they should be a natural part of the Christian life. As we seek God, we will see more and more with our spiritual eyes. Ask God for wisdom and discernment, keeping your eyes and heart focused on Him.

- *Day 28* -

IMAGE: SPRINKLED WITH HIS BLOOD

...And the priest shall make atonement for her, and she shall be clean.
Leviticus 12:8 ESV

I was away at a Christian conference and for three nights, I could not sleep in the hotel room. In fact, I did not even need sleep. The Lord supernaturally caused me to be fully functioning and joyful through-out the days and nights, as I was in deep conversation and commun-ion with Him.

On the third night, in the early morning hours, I had a revelation that I was covered by the truth of His Word, and that it was His blood. Immediately, God gave me a vision of what that looked like. I was laying at Jesus' feet at Calvary. The sky was dark, and the temper-ature was hot and humid. From the cross above, the Lord's blood was falling on me like soft, soft rain, connecting me to Him. As the droplets soaked into my skin, I was receiving His life, His cleansing, His love. It was a beautiful love scene; His death to bring me life! I was experiencing Jesus' sacrifice, and it awakened me to a deeper understanding of His *great love* for me. Thankfulness filled my heart as I was sprinkled with His blood.

...let us approach [God] with a true and sincere heart in unqualified assurance of faith, having had our hearts sprinkled clean from an evil conscience and our bodies washed with pure water.
Hebrews 10:22 AMP

PROMPTS:

Meditate on the blood of Christ and the finished work on the cross. What does it mean to you? How does it affect you? Draw or write.

Using a red pencil or pen, begin to draw droplets that represent the blood of Jesus. With each one, think about Jesus' sacrifice and write what you are thankful to God for (i.e., love, hope, etc.). Pause between each drop and offer up thanks, praise, and worship to God.

_____

_____

_____

_____

_____

_____

_____

_____

_____

_____

- Day 29 -

IMAGE: ENCOURAGING THE HORSE

"So be strong and courageous! Do not be afraid and do not panic...
For the LORD your God will personally go ahead of you. He will
neither fail you nor abandon you."
Deuteronomy 31:6 NLT

I had a quiet moment between conference sessions, so I sat with the
Lord, daydreaming. In the dream, I was a horse; one horse in a herd
of horses. A desire to *run* began to well up inside me. Moving at a
slow trot, I tentatively pulled away from the others and whinnied,
"Come on!" to myself. Soon, I was at a full gallop, delighting in the
running, and heading toward the sunset. My fine fur coat was ready
for the winter weather ahead. I knew that the Lord had prepared me.
He had made me for this!

Sometimes, we need to move on from one thing to another, even
when it's hard. At the time of this journal writing, I was preparing to
leave a church I had been very active in for 20 years. I knew the Lord
had been preparing me, and that this daydream was God's way of
encouraging me to move into the unknown.

I can do all things [which He has called me to do] through Him who
strengthens and empowers me [to fulfill His purpose...I am ready for
anything...through Him who infuses me with inner strength...]
Philippians 4:13 AMP

— Sketch & Write —

PROMPTS:

What encouragement do you need today? Do a search on the internet for encouraging verses from Scripture. Write down a few. Speak them over yourself. Receive encouragement from the Holy Spirit.

Sit quietly with God and daydream with Him. Wait patiently. Draw and write what you see and hear.

_____

_____

_____

_____

_____

_____

_____

_____

Extra: Are you facing a difficult situation? Hearing God doesn't have to be hard. Give your situation to God by faith. Surrender every thought to Him and allow yourself to daydream, to ponder, and to be encouraged. He will strengthen you.

- Day 30 -

IMAGE: HEAPING BURNING COALS

*"...When you walk through the fire, you will not be burned;
the flames will not set you ablaze."*
Isaiah 43:2 NIV

I woke early and talked to God. He wanted me closer than I've ever been before. He wanted deeper intimacy and entwining of our spirits: unity. As part of the process, God showed me that He was heaping burning coals on me in the Spirit. Instead of being hot, though, they felt good, comforting and peaceful. The smoldering embers glowed in reds and oranges. The Lord was burning in and on me, purifying and preparing me for work that He had planned for me to do in the future.

The image God showed me was the spiritual work being done, but in the natural, it did not feel good. I was going through trials and my first instinct was to do everything possible to make the problems stop, but that was not the right attitude. Jesus promises that we will have troubles, but He is with us, in them. We aren't supposed to turn and run. Instead, we should embrace them and count them all joy; we should burn brightly while we are being burnt.

In all this you greatly rejoice, though now for a little while you may have had to suffer grief in all kinds of trials. These have come so that the proven genuineness of your faith—of greater worth than gold, which perishes even though refined by fire—may result in praise, glory and honor when Jesus Christ is revealed.
1 Peter 1:6-7 NIV

187

PROMPTS:

Draw and color heaping burning coals. What purifying work is God doing in you right now?

What trials have you gone through in the past? How has God used them for your good How have they changed you? Write.

_____

_____

_____

_____

_____

_____

_____

_____

_____

- Day 31 -

IMAGE: GET WISDOM

emShme

*"If you need wisdom, ask our generous God,
and he will give it to you..."*
James 1:5 NLT

I was sitting with my arms stretched high, praying and giving thanks to the Lord. I pressed into James 1:5 and asked for wisdom, but it did not reveal itself as I expected. Instead, Wisdom revealed herself as a person. I only caught a glimpse of her in the Spirit, seeing splashes of color as she danced. She wore a skirt of many colors, even colors I didn't recognize. Instinctively, I knew she was artistic and creative and she loved life. I delighted in her and sang of her beauty. I called her to come close to me, for I wanted what she had.

I thought of Solomon. He could have asked God for anything, but he chose wisdom, and God rewarded his choice. When we desire and welcome wisdom, we are seeking God's best. Wisdom is knowing and understanding beyond human capability. It is asking God to impart in us something that expands us and causes us to prosper in all things, and honestly, who doesn't want that?!

*The one who gets wisdom loves life; the one who cherishes
understanding will soon prosper.*
Proverbs 19:8 NIV

PROMPTS:

Read about Wisdom in Proverbs 8 and 9.
Picture Wisdom for yourself.

What does she look like? What are her character traits?
Her personality? Draw or write.

In Proverbs 19:8, how do you think wisdom
prospers a person? Write.

_____

_____

_____

_____

_____

_____

_____

Extra: God seems to love to surprise us and expand our minds. Whatever we think we know, He knows more and He knows better. I love that He wants us to see things in new and deeper ways.

- Day 32 -

IMAGE: POT OF HONEY

"...I would satisfy you with wild honey from the rock."
Psalm 81:16 NLT

Early one morning, I was alone with the Lord. After some time of just being still, I heard Jesus tell me an angel was standing before me, bearing a gift. I held out my hands, in faith, to receive. The angel revealed a long, thin golden teapot and began to pour a thick substance into my hands. It was honey.

What was the meaning of the gift? Was God just reminding me that He is the giver of good things? I felt there was more to it, so I contemplated the word **honey** and I jotted down what came to mind.

- *sweet to the taste*
- *term of endearment*
- *made by many bees working together*
- *source of food*
- *represents provision and abundance*
- *golden in color*
- *has many healing properties*

As I meditated with the Lord, my jotted notes transformed into kingdom words: goodness, love, unity, life, abundance, glory, and healing. I felt my spirit stir as I realized all the words described

Jesus! The image of honey represented Jesus. He is the giver of good things, but He is also the gift that was poured out for us. We just need to receive Him and know there is always more that He wants to give us.

But He poured Himself out *to fill a vessel brand new; a servant in form and a man indeed. The very likeness of humanity, He humbled Himself, obedient to death...*

Philippians 2:7-8 VOICE

PROMPTS:

Hold out your hands and receive the honey that the Lord is pouring out. Be still and receive it. What do you sense? What are you feeling? Write about your experience.

What aspect about honey stands out to you? Draw or write.

How is Jesus the giver of good things to you?
Give specific examples from your life. Write.

_____

_____

_____

_____

_____

_____

_____

- *Day 33* -

IMAGE: JESUS IS THE CURTAIN

emSlune

*...we have confidence to enter the Most Holy Place by the blood of
Jesus, by a new and living way opened for us
through the curtain, that is, His body...*
Hebrews 10:19-20 NIV

I wanted to visualize Hebrews 10:19-20, so I first imagined the tabernacle before Jesus died. Inside the Holy Place was the thick curtain, 30 feet wide x 30 feet high and woven with blue, purple, and scarlet threads. It separated the Most Holy Place, where only the high priest could enter once a year.

The scene changed when Jesus died. The curtain was ripped from the top to the bottom. In my mind, I saw the curtain hanging uselessly from the outermost posts. Standing in its place was Jesus. He became our high priest and He welcomed us to come to the Father. Through Jesus, we now can go boldly to the Most Holy Place and commune with God. Jesus is often referred to as *the way* and *the gate*, but in this image, He is **the curtain** through which we enter.

*Jesus answered, "I am the way and the truth and the life. No one
comes to the Father except through me."*
John 14:6 NIV

PROMPTS:

Pick one of today's verses and meditate on it with the Lord.
Draw or write.

Imagine for yourself that Jesus is standing where the curtain once was. How does He look? What does He say and do? Enter in through Jesus to the Most Holy Place. Describe the experience.

_____

_____

_____

_____

_____

_____

_____

_____

Extra: I am the gate; whoever enters through me will be saved. They will come in and go out, and find pasture. John 19:9 NIV

- *Day 34* -

IMAGE: IN THE KILN

Fire tests the purity of silver and gold, but the LORD tests the heart.
Proverbs 17:3 NLT

I was having a conversation with the Lord while praying in the Spirit, when the Lord asked, "Do you know what you are praying for?" I shook my head in response. He continued, "You are asking for My heart, which is a heart of purity. I am putting your heart through the process by which My all-consuming fire refines out impurities. I examine My work in you and I am well pleased. You are coming out very nicely, like a vase in a kiln."

The Lord assured me that the fire was good and I could withstand the heat. "Don't resist it, but if it ever feels too hot, come to Me. I'll explain. I'll teach. I'll calm. Whatever is needed, I will give it to you. Problems arise when My people don't bring the times of fiery trials to Me; That's what opens doors to the enemy. Your closeness to Me is your protection. It's your covering."

"And I will bring the third part through the fire, and will refine them as silver is refined, and will try them as gold is tried: they shall call on my name, and I will hear them: I will say, It is my people: and they shall say, The Lord is my God."
Zechariah 13:9 KJV

PROMPTS:

How can fire be good? Draw and write.

Remember a time when you felt like you were in the fiery-hot kiln. What was your attitude like? How did you get through it? What did you learn? How did it grow, refine, or purify you? Write.

_____

_____

_____

_____

_____

_____

_____

Extra: The next time you are in a trial, ask God what He wants to do in and through it. Turn the negative situation around and look to see how God is working. When you don't understand, ask Him. Wait patiently. He will answer.

- Day 35 -

IMAGE: INSIDE GOD'S HEART

But the one who joins himself to the Lord is one spirit with Him.
1 Corinthians 6:17 ESV

While upstairs, sitting in bed, I was spending time alone with God and He said, "Look into My heart." So, in my mind and by faith, I imagined myself putting my head into His heart, and I looked inside. The chamber was like polished crystal-metal, so clean and pure, and so unlike a fleshly human heart, I thought, *His heart is not like our heart.* The smooth surfaces gleamed with hints of colors, reflecting glory and holiness.

Then, my whole body was taken inside God's heart. I stood there in awe. I was in God, surrounded by the beautiful chamber walls. I grasped for words to describe what I was seeing and feeling. Words like: *calmness, stillness, life, vibrancy, beauty, organic, and flowing* came, but they were poor substitutes because no language could adequately describe such a mystery.

Then, I prayed in the Spirit and God interpreted for me. "You are asking to be a part of My heart. You desire what I desire. You want to be like David, a man after My own heart. I grant that request. I purify you. I set you apart. I call you closer. I have shown you My own heart. I invite you to dwell here in My holy habitation." All I could do was bow down in wonder and love. I was overwhelmed by His greatness and completely undone, kneeling there inside God's heart.

My people will abide in a peaceful habitation, in secure dwellings,
and in quiet resting places.
Isaiah 32:18 ESV

PROMPTS:

Sit quietly with God. Meditate on His heart. What is He telling you? Showing you? Draw or write.

Do you need peace and rest right now? Meditate on Isaiah 32:18 and write out a prayer to God.

_____

_____

_____

_____

_____

_____

_____

_____

- Day 36 -

IMAGE: ANGEL OF PROMOTION

emme

God blessed them and said..., "Be fruitful and increase in number;
fill the earth and subdue it. Rule over the fish in the sea and the birds
in the sky and over every living creature that moves on the ground."
Genesis 1:28 NIV

One Sunday morning I was visiting a church and sensed an angel's
presence, so I asked the Lord about him. Jesus informed me that he
was an angel of promotion. I looked in the Spirit and the angel had a
box of promotional goodies that he was handing out to people. When
he got to me, he gave me a blue and green stress ball that looked like
planet earth. I almost laughed out loud in the middle of the service. I
thought, *Really Lord, a stress ball,* but the Holy Spirit quickly
corrected me with revelation.

God has given humankind the world to have dominion over. The ball
was not a fun, clever trinket. It represented serious business. All
authority and power are given to us by Father God. Through Jesus,
we are instructed to live out Kingdom Life here on Earth, to go and
do the things Jesus did.

As I sat holding the invisible mini-world, I no longer heard the
pastor's sermon. I was thinking instead of what I needed to do with
my new promotion. Christianity is not supposed to be passive; Jesus
calls us into action. He created the earth, telling us to rule and reign

and to be His ambassadors to the world. We are to do all that He did, and even greater things than He did.

And Jesus came and said to them, "All authority in heaven and on earth has been given to me. Go therefore and make disciples of all nations, baptizing them in the name of the Father and of the Son and of the Holy Spirit, teaching them to observe all that I have commanded you..."
Matthew 28:18-20 ESV

PROMPTS:

Daydream with God. If the angel of promotion visited you, what would he give you? Ask the Holy Spirit. Draw or write.

Meditate on the words: authority and dominion.
What is our role on earth? Write.

- *Day 37* -

IMAGE: MISSING A FEATHER

Saul's son Jonathan, David's friend, had a son named Mephibosheth who was unable to use his feet. When he was only five, the news of his father and grandfather's defeat came from Jezreel. In her rush to flee, his nurse grabbed him up, and Mephibosheth fell; he had been lame ever since.
2 Samuel 4:4 VOICE

I was outside on my birthday, and a large crow flew over me. He was missing a feather on his right wing and it caused a large gap, but it did not hinder him from flying. I thought about how this image applied to my own life. I missed out on some things in my childhood due to mental illness in a family member, but the Lord has healed and restored many things, and no deficiency will stop me from flying!

Later that same day, the Lord expanded my thinking even further by showing me three birds in the sky. They were so high up, they looked like mere specks. They weren't just flying, they were soaring. I thought of my relationship with God (Father, Son, and Holy Spirit). I wanted to experience that level of freedom and joy with Him. So, I said, "Yes, Lord, I want that! I don't just want to fly. I want to soar with You!"

…And David said, "Mephibosheth!…I will show you kindness for the sake of your father Jonathan, and I will restore to you all the land of Saul your father, and you shall eat at my table always."
2 Samuel 9:6-7 ESV

PROMPTS:

Draw a feather that represents what is missing for you (loss, rejection, hurt, disappointment, etc.) and write an honest letter to Jesus about it. Then, give the feather to Him to restore.

Meditate on today's Scriptures about Mephibosheth. Can you relate to his story? Remember a struggle that you had in the past that God turned into good. Write.

_____

_____

_____

_____

_____

_____

_____

Extra: I had bottled up my emotions, vowing to never cry again, because of hurts and disappointments, but Jesus taught me to give those things to Him. Over many years, He would bring up memories to be dealt with. As I let each thing go, as I forgave, my heart healed. Jesus was so sweet, and tender, and gentle, I learned I could trust Him with my heart.

.

- Day 38 -

IMAGE: THREE KINDS OF CANDLES

"If thy whole body therefore be full of light, having no part dark, the whole shall be full of light, as when the bright shining of a candle doth give thee light."
Luke 11:36 KJV

As I prayed, in my mind, I saw three small candles. The first was an unlit candle with a charred wick. The second was a lit candle with a healthy flame. The third was a melting, oozing-wax candle that had been blowtorched. The Lord told me it was a parable in which each candle represented Christians walking out their faith.

Some, like the first candle, burned out quickly or were stifled by fear, never sharing the light or fire. They held so much potential, but they were like the one hiding their light under a basket (Matthew 5:15). The second, lit candle represented the Christian who shares God's light, fire, and love with one person at a time. This person takes time to love, hug, share, heal, feed, clothe, teach, and care for others. The third, torched candle represented the Christian who burned every-thing in their path due to overzealousness, immaturity, impatience, pride, or lack of wisdom or love. This kind caused people to get hurt.

The Lord concluded by saying, "It's perfectly simple, don't make it hard." I smiled at that because it was clear we are to be like the second candle who burns steadily, releasing light and warmth, and igniting others with our flame. I pray, *Lord, help us to be that kind of candle.*

"And you, beloved, are the light of the world…"
Matthew 5:14 VOICE

PROMPTS:

Which candle represents you right now? Draw or write. Pray for God's help to be the light of the world.

Look up parables in the Bible. Which parable speaks to you the most? Draw or write.

_____

_____

_____

_____

_____

_____

_____

_____

Extra: Some of the parables: The Sower, The Mustard Seed, The Pearl, The Lost Sheep, The Prodigal Son, The Unforgiving Servant, The Good Samaritan, The Wise and Foolish Builders, The Ten Virgins, The Persistent Widow.

- Day 39 -

IMAGE: EAGLES OR CHICKENS

But those who trust in the LORD will find new strength. They will soar high on wings like eagles...
Isaiah 40:31 NLT

In the midst of worship, I saw an image of a flying eagle in my mind. Then, I saw another image of chickens on the ground. The message was simple: Some soar, but others peck in the dust. I asked myself, *Where is my vantage point? Is it from the heavens or is it in the dirt?*

I thought of the times when I did not believe in God's best for me - when I focused on my small bank account, or when I accepted pain in my body. I cannot go back there, to pecking in the dirt. I wanted to believe what the Word of God said. I wanted to soar. Jesus taught us to pray, "...on earth as it is in heaven..." (Matthew 6:10). Why pray that way if we can't have it, if it's not attainable? I recommitted myself to trusting in what God says, and settling for nothing less.

Then I heard the Lord say, "Keep your mind on things above (Colossians 3:2). Your feet are on the ground, but your head should be in the clouds. My intent for humanity is greatness, for I made you in My image and likeness. I did not make you to fall, to fail, to be sick, or to struggle. I made you to walk with Me, to prosper, to have peace, to love and to be loved, and to have joy. Through My Son, I restore all things back to the way they were meant to be."

He will make you the head, not the tail; you'll always be on top and never on the bottom—if you'll just listen to the commands I'm giving you today from the Eternal your God, and obey them carefully.
Deuteronomy 28:13 VOICE

PROMPTS:

What is your current vantage point? Are you soaring or pecking?
Draw or write and then pray.

What do you need to trust God for? Pick one verse from the Bible to
be your promise from God. Focus on it day and night, till you are
trusting. Refuse to focus on the issue or problem.

_____

_____

_____

_____

_____

_____

_____

_____

- Day 40 -

IMAGE: LEARNING TO PADDLE

Whether you turn to the right or to the left, your ears will hear a voice behind you, saying, "This is the way..."
Isaiah 30:21 NIV

I was camping for the weekend at a state park, and in the heat of the summer day, I decided to go back to the cabin for some quiet time with the Lord. As I rested, the Lord brought my early-morning kayaking on the lake to mind. He began to speak to me using that image. "Your life is like paddling on a lake. Some parts are shallow, and some parts are deep. You often live life not knowing where you are going, but know this: I am with you" (Isaiah 41:1). God asked me, "Do you love Me?"

I answered, "Yes, Lord!"

"Then know, I am working all things for your good (Romans 8:28). You are moving through the water, paddling forward. Do not be discouraged if you are still in shallow waters, learning to paddle. It is a good place to be. Give thanks at every stage of the journey. My angels surround you – they do indeed 'camp' around you." (Psalm 34:7).

Do not despise these small beginnings for the Lord rejoices to see the work begin.
Zechariah 4:10 NLT

PROMPTS:

What part of the lake is your life currently in (shallow or deep)?
Draw or write.

What trial have you "paddled" through? Draw a paddle and write the
trial on it. Describe how God helped you through it.

Sit and meditate with God. Ask Him what encouragement He has for
you in this season of life. Write what you hear.

_____

_____

_____

_____

_____

_____

_____

_____

Final Thoughts from Dawn

Dear Friend,

Thank you for reading and being on this journey with me! I wish I could sit down with you in person, over a cup of coffee or tea, to encourage you to keep pressing into God. I know you have encountered Him in your devotion time. As I finished the manuscript revisions, I realized the closing chapter of this book should be a personal letter to you. Here are the things God put on my heart to share.

SEEK GOD

Seek God early in the day and seek Him often! Seek Him in His Word, the Bible and seek Him wherever you go. Look for Him in the clouds, in song lyrics, in a person's smile. Continuously turn your thoughts to Him. Abide in Him and He will abide in you (John 15:4).

BE FILLED UP

Be filled with the Holy Spirit. Ask God to fill you to overflowing, so you are bursting with His power and life, able to overcome every adversity in Christ Jesus.

ASK AND STEP

What are the desires of your heart? Where is God leading you? I have a sign in my office that reads: *Every great journey begins with one single yet brave little step.* Take a step, even a small one, in the direction that you feel God is drawing you.

TAKE COURAGE

God gave me a word one year -- "courage." At the time, I wasn't sure I wanted a word like that. It sounded hard, scary, and impossible. But now, I realize courage has to do with the development of the heart and living in fullness in Him. In Jesus, we have courage because He is our courage. It's not me being courageous because honestly, I'm not. But, in Christ, I can do all things. He strengthens me (Philippians 4:13). So, I pass the word "courage" on to you. Will you take it?

EXPAND THE KINGDOM

God is constantly expanding His Kingdom. He never wants us to quit or be stagnant, but instead wants us to grow what He gives us. What started out as my personal devotions, the images and meditations from my journal, God wanted to expand. He told me to share them because they weren't just for me. He will ask you to do your part too, for He has a plan for your life that only you can fulfill. He wants all to be saved (and that includes wholeness, healing, deliverance, as well as being right with God). He wants all to be united in Christ Jesus.

He wants you.

He calls you.

You are courageous. You are loved by God.

I bless you in the name of Jesus. Be fruitful and multiply in all you do.

Much Love,

Dawn

PS: My heart's desire is that the devotions and prompts have spurred you on! Maybe they were challenging? How has the book impacted you? How has God worked through it? Would you share your story? I'd love to hear and be able to cheer you on your journey.

PPS: If you enjoyed this book, please leave a review on Amazon. I read every review, and they help new readers discover the book. Thank you!

About the Author

Dawn Hamsher is a writer, dreamer, and encourager who calls women to come closer to Jesus. Her endearing demeanor resonates in her writing, drawing readers to seek God alongside her. For the past 15 years, she's led Bible studies and retreats and has been whole-heartedly going after God with her trusty journal by her side. These years of meditating on Scripture and spending many hours getting to know God have resulted in dreams and visions and even healing. Her heart's desire is for people to know Jesus intimately and to experience His healing power.

By day, Dawn is an IT Specialist, but by night, you might find her praying, speaking, blogging, or meeting a friend over coffee. Once a week, she plays with clay (hubby calls it pottering), making fun and quirky slab-work pottery. Dawn also enjoys camping and long walks. She lives in Chambersburg, PA with her husband, Toby, their adult daughter, Gillian, and her sidekick, a toothless cat named Pippa, who loves belly rubs.

DawnHamsher.com
www.facebook.com/dawnhamsher1

www.ingramcontent.com/pod-product-compliance
Lightning Source LLC
Chambersburg PA
CBHW070917120626
46546CB00001B/305